What An
A Book of R

D1577717

By Jennifer M Edwards

Copyright © 2012 by Jennifer M Edwards
All rights reserved.

No part of this publication may be reproduced, stored in a retrieval
system, or transmitted in any form or by any other means
electronic, mechanical, photocopying or otherwise, without prior
permission from the author.

This book is sold subject to the condition that it shall not, by way of
trade or otherwise, be lent, re-sold, hired out or otherwise
circulated without the author's prior consent in any form of binding
or cover other than that in which it is published and without a
similar condition including this condition being imposed on the
subsequent purchaser.

Riddles

1
It is greater than God and more evil than the devil. The poor have it, the rich need it and if you eat it you'll die. What is it?

2
I am the beginning of the end, and the end of time and space. I am essential to creation, and I surround every place. What am I?

3
What always runs but never walks, often murmurs, never talks, has a bed but never sleeps, has a mouth but never eats?

4
I never was, am always to be.
No one ever saw me, nor ever will.
And yet I am the confidence of all,
To live and breathe on this terrestrial ball.
What am I?

5
At night they come without being fetched. By day they are lost without being stolen. What are they?

6
There was a green house. Inside the green house there was a white house. Inside the white house there was a red house. Inside the red house there were lots of babies. What is it?

Answers

1

Nothing. Nothing is greater than God, nothing is more evil than the devil, the poor have nothing, the rich need nothing and if you eat nothing you'll die.

2

The letter 'e'. End, time, space, Every placE.

3

A river.

4

Tomorrow or the future.

5

The stars.

6

A watermelon.

Riddles

7
What is in seasons, seconds, centuries and minutes but not in decades, years or days?

8
The person who makes it, sells it. The person who buys it never uses it and the person who uses it doesn't know they are. What is it?

9
The more you have of it, the less you see. What is it?

10
What has a head, a tail, is brown, and has no legs?

11
What English word has three consecutive double letters?

12
What's black when you get it, red when you use it, and white when you're all through with it?

13
You throw away the outside and cook the inside. Then you eat the outside and throw away the inside. What did you eat?

Answers

7
The letter 'n'.

8
A coffin.

9
Darkness.

10
A penny.

11
Bookkeeper.

12
Charcoal.

13
An ear of corn.

Riddles

14
I am always hungry,
I must always be fed,
The finger I touch,
Will soon turn red.
What am I?

15
Ripped from my mother's womb,
Beaten and burned,
I become a blood thirsty killer.
What am I?

16
I know a word of letters three. Add two, and fewer there will be.
What word am I?

17
I give you a group of three. One is sitting down, and will never get
up. The second eats as much as is given to him, yet is always
hungry. The third goes away and never returns.
What are we?

18
I have four legs but no tail. Usually I am heard only at night.
What am I?

Answers

14
Fire.

15
Iron ore.

16
Few.

17
Stove, fire, smoke.

18
A frog. The frog is an amphibian in the order Anura (meaning "tailless") and usually makes noises at night during its mating season.

Riddles

19
When young, I am sweet in the sun.
When middle-aged, I make you gay.
When old, I am valued more than ever.
What am I?

20
All about, but cannot be seen,
Can be captured, cannot be held,
No throat, but can be heard.
What am I?

21
If you break me
I do not stop working,
If you touch me
I may be snared,
If you lose me
Nothing will matter.
What am I?

22
Until I am measured
I am not known,
Yet how you miss me
When I have flown.
What am I?

Answers

19
Wine.

20
The wind.

21
Your heart.

22
Time.

Riddles

23

I drive men mad
For love of me,
Easily beaten,
Never free.
What am I?

24

When set loose, I fly away,
Never cursed, as when I go astray.
What am I?

25

Lighter than what
I am made of,
More of me is hidden
Than is seen.
What am I?

26

Each morning I appear
To lie at your feet,
All day I will follow
No matter how fast you run,
Yet I nearly perish
In the midday sun.
What am I?

Answers

23
Gold.

24
A fart.

25
Iceberg.

26
Shadow.

Riddles

27

My life can be measured in hours,
I serve by being devoured.
Thin, I am quick
Fat, I am slow
Wind is my foe.
What am I?

28

I am seen in the water
If seen in the sky,
I am in the rainbow,
A jay's feather,
And lapis lazuli.
What am I?

29

Glittering points
That downward thrust,
Sparkling spears
That never rust.
What am I?

30

You heard me before, yet you hear me again,
Then I die, 'till you call me again.
What am I?

Answers

27
A candle.

28
Blue.

29
Icicle.

30
An echo.

Riddles

31
Three lives have I.
Gentle enough to soothe the skin,
Light enough to caress the sky,
Hard enough to crack rocks.
What am I?

32
At the sound of me,
Men may dream
Or stamp their feet
At the sound of me,
Women may laugh
Or sometimes weep.
What am I?

33
What does man love more than life
Fear more than death or mortal strife
What the poor have, the rich require,
and what contented men desire,
What the miser spends and the spendthrift saves
And all men carry to their graves?

34
I build up castles, I tear down mountains.
I make some men blind, I help others to see.
What am I?

Answers

31
Water.

32
Music.

33
Nothing.

34
Sand.

Riddles

35
Two in a corner,
1 in a room,
0 in a house,
But 1 in a shelter.
What am I?

36
Five hundred begins it, five hundred ends it,
Five in the middle is seen;
First of all figures, the first of all letters,
Take up their stations between.
Join all together, and then you will bring
Before you the name of an eminent king.
Who am I?

37
It cannot be seen, it weighs nothing, but when put into a barrel, it makes it lighter. What is it?

38
How far will a blind dog walk into a forest?

39
What happens when you throw a yellow rock into a purple stream?

40
What starts with a T, ends with a T, and has "T" in it?

Answers

35
The letter 'r'.

36
DAVID (Roman numerals).

37
A hole.

38
Halfway. After he gets halfway, he's walking out of the forest.

39
It makes a splash.

40
A teapot.

Riddles

41

Whoever makes it, tells it not.
Whoever takes it, knows it not.
Whoever knows it, wants it not.
What is it?

42

I am, in truth, a yellow fork
From tables in the sky
By inadvertent fingers dropped
The awful cutlery.
Of mansions never quite disclosed
And never quite concealed
The apparatus of the dark
To ignorance revealed.
(-- Emily Dickenson)
What am I?

43

You saw me where I never was and where I could not be. And yet
within that very place, my face you often see. What am I?

44

Say my name and I disappear. What am I?

45

What is it that after you take away the whole,
some still remains?

Answers

41
Counterfeit money.

42
Lightning.

43
A reflection.

44
Silence.

45
Wholesome.

Riddles

46

A box without hinges, lock or key, yet golden treasure lies within. What is it?

47

Forward I'm heavy, but backwards I'm not. What am I?

48

Why doesn't a mountain covered with snow catch cold?

49

I can be long, or I can be short.
I can be grown, and I can be bought.
I can be painted, or left bare.
I can be round, or square.
What am I?

50

One by one we fall from heaven,
Down into the depths of past.
And our world is ever upturned,
So that yet some time we'll last.
What am I?

51

Kings and queens may cling to power, and the jester's got his call.
But, as you may all discover, the common one outranks them all.
What am I?

Answers

46
An egg.

47
Ton.

48
Because it has a snowcap.

49
A fingernail.

50
Sands in an hourglass.

51
An ace (in a deck of cards).

Riddles

52

I drift forever with the current,
Down these long canals they've made.
Tame, yet wild, I run elusive,
Multitasking to your aid.
Before I came, the world was darker,
Colder, sometimes, rougher, true.
But though I might make living easy,
I'm good at killing people too.
What am I?

53

Reaching stiffly for the sky,
I bare my fingers when it's cold.
In warmth I wear an emerald glove,
And in between I dress in gold.
What am I?

54

Every dawn begins with me,
At dusk I'll be the first you see.
And daybreak couldn't come without,
What midday centers all about.
Daises grow from me, I'm told,
And when I come, I end all cold.
But in the sun I won't be found,
Yet still, each day I'll be around.
What am I?

Answers

52

Electricity (or lightning).

53

A deciduous tree.

54

The letter 'd'.

Riddles

55

Kings and lords and Christians raised them,
Since they stand for higher powers.
Yet few of them would stand, I'm certain,
If women ruled this world of ours.
What am I?

56

Soft and fragile is my skin,
I get my growth in mud.
I'm dangerous as much as pretty,
For if not careful, I draw blood.
What am I?

57

Three brothers share a family sport:
A non-stop marathon
The oldest one is fat and short
And trudges slowly on
The middle brother's tall and slim
And keeps a steady pace
The youngest runs just like the wind,
A-speeding through the race
"He's young in years, we let him run,"
The other brothers say
"'Cause though he's surely number one,
He's second, in a way."
What are we?

Answers

55

A tower.

56

A thorn.

57

The hands on a clock (hour, minute, second)

Riddles

58

It's true I bring serenity,
And hang around the stars,
But yet I live in misery;
You'll find me behind bars,
With thieves and villains I consort,
In prison I'll be found,
But I would never go to court,
Unless there's more than one. What am I?

59

I am a box that holds keys without locks,
yet they can unlock your soul. What am I?

60

There is one word that stands the test of time and holds fast to the
center of everything. Though everyone will try at least once in their
life to move around this word, but in fact, unknowingly, they use it
every moment of the day. Young or old, awake or in sleep, human
or animal, this word stands fast. It belongs to everyone, to all living
things, but no one can master it. What word am I?

61

My first is twice in apple but not once in tart.
My second is in liver but not in heart.
My third is in giant and also in ghost.
Whole I'm best, when I am roast.
What am I?

Answers

58
The letter 's'.

59
A piano.

60
Gravity.

61
A pig.

Riddles

62

What gets wetter as it dries?

63

When you went into the woods you got me.
You hated me yet you wanted to find me.
You went home with me because you couldn't find me.
What was it?

64

This is a most unusual paragraph. How quickly can you find out
what is so unusual about it? It looks so ordinary you'd think
nothing was wrong with it - and in fact, nothing is wrong with it. It is
unusual though. Why? Study it, think about it, and you may find
out. Try to do it without coaching. If you work at it for a bit it will
dawn on you. So jump to it and try your skill at figuring it out. Good
luck - don't blow your cool!

65

An iron horse with a flaxen tail.
The faster the horse runs,
the shorter his tail becomes.
What is it?

66

You have to travel far before you turn it over. What is it?

Answers

62
A towel.

63
A splinter.

64
The most common letter in the English language, the letter 'e', is not found in the entire paragraph

65
A needle and thread.

66
An odometer.

Riddles

67
A mile from end to end, yet as close to as a friend, a precious commodity, freely given, seen on the dead and on the living. Found on the rich, poor, short and tall, but shared among children most of all. What is it?

68
I'm full of holes, yet I'm full of water. What am I?

69
Four of us are in your field
But our differences keep us at yield
First, a one that is no fool
Though he resembles a gardener's tool
Next, one difficult to split in two
And a girl once had one as big as her shoe
Then, to the mind, one's a lovely bonder
And truancy makes it grow fonder
Last, a stem connecting dots of three
Knowing all this, what are we?

70
A man went to the hardware store to buy items for his house.
1 would cost $0.25
12 would cost $0.50
122 would cost $0.75
When he left the store he had spent $0.75.
What did he buy?

Answers

67
A smile.

68
A sponge.

69
The four suits in a deck of standard playing cards.
The Spade is a gardener's tool.
The Diamond is the hardest gem to break.
"Little Girl and Queen" is a Mother Goose rhyme, in which the Queen gave the girl a large diamond for picking the Queen some roses.
The Heart bonds with the mind to form love.
Absence makes the heart grow fonder.
The Club, or Clover, is three dots connected around a stem.

70
House numbers.

Riddles

71
I am a word of meanings three.
Three ways of spelling me there be.
The first is an odour, a smell if you will.
The second some money, but not in a bill.
The third is past tense,
A method of passing things on or around.
Can you tell me now, what these words are,
that have the same sound?

72
It's red, blue, purple and green, no one can reach it, not even the queen. What is it?

73
What question can you never honestly answer yes to?

74
What has a neck and no head, two arms but no hands?

75
Feed me and I live, give me drink and I die. What am I?

76
What begins and has no end?
What is the ending of all that begins?

Answers

71
Scent, cent, sent.

72
A rainbow.

73
Are you asleep? (or dead)

74
A shirt (or sweater, jacket, etc.)

75
Fire.

76
Death or decay.

Riddles

77

What makes a loud noise when changing its jacket and becomes larger but weighs less?

78

The more you take, the more you leave behind. What am I?

79

I am a word of 5 letters and people eat me. If you remove the first letter I become a form of energy. Remove the first two and I'm needed to live. Scramble the last 3 and you can drink me. What word am I?

80

Before any changes I'm a garlic or spice. My first is altered and I'm a hand-warming device. My second is changed and I'm trees in full bloom. The next letter change makes a deathly old tomb. Change the fourth to make a fruit of the vine. Change the last for a chart plotted with lines. What was I? What did I become? What did I turn out to be?

81

A woman shoots her husband, then holds him under water for five minutes. Finally, she hangs him. Five minutes later they enjoy a wonderful dinner together. How can this be?

82

What holds two people together but touches only one?

Answers

77
Popcorn.

78
Footsteps.

79
Wheat, heat, eat, tea.

80
Clove, glove, grove, grave, grape, graph

81
She took a photo of him and developed it in the dark room

82
A wedding ring.

Riddles

83

Alive without breath, as cold as death,
Clad in mail never clinking, never thirsty, ever drinking.
What am I?

84

I can always go up, never down,
I can always turn left, never right,
I am always hot when I'm cold.
What am I?

85

A cowboy rides into town on Friday, stays for three days and
leaves on Friday. How did he do it?

86

What has roots that nobody sees,
Is taller than trees,
Up, up it goes, yet it never grows?

87

This thing all things devours,
Birds, beasts, trees, and flowers.
Gnaws iron bites steel,
Grinds hard stones to meal,
Slays king, ruins town,
And beats high mountain down.
What am I?

Answers

83
A fish.

84
A ski lift.

85
The horse's name is Friday.

86
A mountain.

87
Time.

Riddles

88

It cannot be seen, it cannot be felt,
Cannot be heard, cannot be smelt,
Lies behind stars and under hills,
And empty holes it fills.
Comes first follows after,
Ends life kills laughter.
What am I?

89

A man is born in 1946 and dies in 1947, yet he was 86 years old.
How is that possible?

90

I go in hard.
I come out soft.
You blow me hard.
What am I?

91

Two words is my answer. In order to keep me,
you have to give me. What am I?

92

If you drop me I'm sure to crack but give me a smile and I'll always
smile back. What am I?

Answers

88
Darkness.

89
He was born in room # 1946 of the hospital and died in room # 1947 86 years later

90
Gum.

91
Your word.

92
A mirror.

Riddles

93

What does this represent?
Standing
World

94

What does this represent?
Wear
Black

95

Old Mother Twitchet had one eye,
and a long tail that she let fly.
And every time she went through a gap,
she left some tail in the trap.
What are we?

96

Little Miss Eticote,
In her white petticoat,
And a red nose,
The longer she stands,
The shorter she grows.
What am I?

97

Remove six letters from this sequence to reveal a familiar English
word. BSAINXLEATNTEARS.

Answers

93

Standing on top of the world.

94

Black underwear.

95

A needle and thread.

96

A candle.

97

BANANA (Removed SIX LETTERS)

Riddles

98

What force and strength cannot get through,
I, with a gentle touch, can do.
And many in the street would stand,
Were I not a friend at hand.
What am I?

99

Round like an apple, deep like a cup,
Yet all the king's horses cannot pull it up.
What am I?

100

Thirty white horses on a red hill,
First champ, then stamp, and then stand still.
What are we?

101

Black we are and much admired,
Men seek us if they are tired,
We tire the horse, comfort man,
Guess this riddle if you can.

102

Weight in my belly, trees on my back;
Nails in my ribs, feet I do lack.
What am I?

Answers

98
A key.

99
A well.

100
Your teeth.

101
Coal.

102
A ship.

Riddles

103

Only one color, but not one size,
Stuck at the bottom, yet easily flies;
Present in sun, but not in rain;
Doing no harm, and feeling no pain.
What am I?

104

What lives in the corner but travels the world?

105

I'm white, I'm round, but not always around. Sometimes you see
me, sometimes you don't. What am I?

106

There are two meanings to me. With one I may need to be broken,
with the other I hold on. My favorite characteristic is my charming
dimple. What am I?

107

Toss me out of the window,
You'll find a grieving wife,
Pull me back but through the door,
And watch someone give life!
What am I?

108

What has a head, one arm, one leg and a round bottom?

Answers

103
A shadow.

104
A postage stamp.

105
The moon.

106
A tie.

107
The letter 'n' (widow, donor)

108
A handicapped parking sign.

Riddles

109

I have an end but no beginning, a home but no family, a space without a room. I never speak but there is no word I cannot make. What am I?

110

I go in dry and come out wet, the longer I'm in, the stronger I get. What am I?

111

In the day I stand tall in a white petticoat. By evening I'm in my short black dress. What am I?

112

I cannot be other than what I am,
Until the man who made me dies.
Power and glory will fall to me finally,
Only when he last closes his eyes.
What am I?

113

Two in a whole and four in a pair,
And six in a trio you see,
And eight's a quartet but what you must get,
Is the name that fits just one of me?

114

What asks no questions but receives lots of answers?

Answers

109
A keyboard.

110
A tea bag.

111
The wick of a candle.

112
A prince.

113
A half.

114
A phone or doorbell.

Riddles

115
In the night a mountain, in the morning a meadow. What am I?

116
What goes up but never comes down?

117
Three little letters, a paradox to some.
The worse that it is, the better it becomes.
What am I?

118
I am in a house with no doors. There are people inside
but no reply. What am I?

119
I hide but my head is outside. What am I?

120
When a bird flies over the ocean a part of the body touches the
water but doesn't get wet. What part is it?

121
I appear in the morning but am always there.
You can never see me though I am everywhere.
By night I am gone, though I sometimes never was.
Nothing can defeat me but I am easily gone.
What am I?

Answers

115
A bed.

116
Your age.

117
Pun.

118
A fish.

119
A nail.

120
The shadow.

121
Sunlight.

Riddles

122

In the marble walls as white as milk,
Lined with skin as soft as silk,
Within a fountain crystal clear,
A golden apple does appear.
No doors are there to this stronghold
Yet thieves break in and steal the gold.
What am I?

123

I live in a busy place in the city,
I'll let you stay with me for awhile,
If you don't feed me,
I can get you into trouble.
What am I?

124

The first is a person who lives in disguise
Who deals in secrets and tells nothing but lies.
Then think of a letter that's last to mend
The middle of middle and end of end.
Now think of a sound which is often heard
In search of every unknown word.
Put it together and answer me this,
Which creature would you be unwilling to kiss?

Answers

122
An egg or egg yolk.

123
A parking meter.

124
Spy, d, er, creature: spider

Riddles

125
The first 2 letters of this English word refer to a male, the first three refer to a female, the first 4 to a great man and the whole word is a great woman. What word am I?

126
What word is the same written forward,
backward and upside down?

127
What instrument can make any sound and be heard but not touched or seen?

128
What surrounds the world, yet dwells within a thimble?

129
I am whole but incomplete. I have no eyes, yet I see. You can see,
and see right through me.
My largest part is one fourth of what I once was.
What am I?

130
I am big and mighty, and scared of sharp objects.
I feed everyone and watch people go by.
I have my feet stuck and hate talking with my big mouth.
What am I?

Answers

125
Heroine (he, her, hero).

126
Noon.

127
Your voice.

128
Space.

129
A skeleton.

130
A tree.

Riddles

131
I wear a red robe,
With staff in hand,
And a stone in my throat.
What am I?

132
I have a mouth on my head and eat everything. What am I?

133
Gets rid of bad ones,
Short and tall,
Tightens when used,
One size fits all.
What am I?

134
What comes in different sizes, different colors and
different shapes?

135
I met an old man on London bridge,
As the sun set on the ridge,
He tipped his hat and drew his name,
And cheated at the guessing game.
What was the man's name?

Answers

131
A cherry.

132
A backpack.

133
A noose.

134
A jigsaw puzzle piece.

135
Andrew.

Riddles

136

yyyy U R, yyyy U B, I C U R y y 4 ?
What word belongs in place of the question mark?

137

I live above a star but never burn.
I have 11 neighbors but they never turn.
My initials are p, q, r and sometimes s.
What am I?

138

Tear one off and scratch my head. What once was red is black instead. What am I?

139

She awakes, I touch her and she spreads her legs apart. We are both nervous but I continue. Finally the white liquid comes. What happened?

140

Tall in the morning, short at noon, gone at night but I'll be back soon. What am I?

141

What four letters frighten a thief?

142

How is the letter T like an island?

Answers

136
Me (wise you are, wise you be, I see you are too wise for me)

137
Number 7 on a phone keypad

138
A match.

139
Milking a cow.

140
A shadow.

141
OICU (oh, I see you).

142
It's in the middle of water

Riddles

143

What come once in a minute, twice in a moment but not once in a thousand years?

144

If you have it, you want to share it.
If you share it, you don't have it.
What is it?

145

Where can you find a 3 foot ruler?

146

What falls but never breaks and breaks but never falls?

147

What do you throw out to use and take in when you're done?

148

Voiceless it cries, wingless flutters, toothless bites,
mouthless mutters. What am I?

149

The thunder comes before the lightning,
And the lightning comes before the cloud,
The rain dries all the land it touches,
Wrapping the earth in a blood red shroud.
What am I?

Answers

143
The letter 'm'.

144
A secret.

145
At a yard sale.

146
Night and day.

147
An anchor.

148
The wind.

149
A volcano.

Riddles

150
A word, I know, six letters it contains, subtract just one and twelve remains. What word am I?

151
People need me but they always give me away. What am I?

152
I crawl on the earth and rise on a pillar. What am I?

153
What kind of pet always stays on the floor?

154
I'm found on a hand and also a tree,
You'll find me on Sunday, occasionally,
Records, pictures, islands and brew,
From August to Wolfgang and Sago for you.
What am I?

155
Snake coiled round and round,
Snake deep below the ground,
Snake that's never had a head,
Snake that binds but not with dread.
What am I?

Answers

150
Dozens, dozen.

151
Money.

152
A shadow.

153
Carpet.

154
Palm.

155
A rope.

Riddles

156

I have palms but not on hands,
I offer foods from distant lands,
When at my peak you'll see me smoke,
I'm famous for my friendly folk,
My flowers grow and yet they lay,
There's fire where a man will play,
I'm sure you know we're family,
You're welcome to come stay with me.
What am I?

157

The answer to each clue is a single, 100-point word, or a word
whose letters add up to 100, with a = 1, b = 2, etc.
i. Peanut butter tastes like this.
ii. The hat a Dad wears.
iii. To fire a chef,
iv. A smart timepiece.
v. Figured it out again.
vi. Where a kid can sleep.
vii. The magical fruit leaves you doing this.
viii. Betrayed for this much silver.
ix. A baked good that is height challenged.
x. A sticky way to neaten your hair.

158

What type of house weighs the least?

Answers

156
Hawaii.

157
i. nutty
ii. fatherhood
iii. cookout
iv. clockwise
v. resolved
vi. boycott
vii. tooting
viii. thirty
ix. shortcake
x. honeycomb

158
A lighthouse.

Riddles

159
What do you not want to have and not want to lose?

160
I belong to you, but am used more by others. What am I?

161
What do horses, sleep and dreams have in common?

162
Which tree is the most difficult to get along with?

163
Boys use it, girls like it, parents hate it.
What is this 5-letter word?

164
Stars awash in a sheen of light
It calls out loud in vile delight.
Listeners endure in fright.
Vicious brute that reigns at night,
Evil whelped of heinous bite,
Renewed by wax, it regains might.
A leading way to slay the beast,
Get the hidden weapon thus released.
What am I?

Answers

159
A lawsuit.

160
Your name.

161
Nightmares.

162
A crabtree.

163
Phone.

164
A werewolf (vulnerable to silver bullets)

Riddles

165

Halo of water, tongue of wood,
Skin of stone, long I've stood.
My fingers short reach to the sky,
Inside my heart men live and die.
What am I?

166

I am in the sky but also in the ground. When you study me, no
matter how long, I will always end with an f. I may be in your yard
but not in your house. What am I?

167

I spit like bacon, am made with an egg,
I have plenty of backbone but lack good legs,
I peel like an onion but still remain whole,
I'm long like a flagpole, yet fit in a hole
What am I?

168

The more you take from me, the bigger I get. What am I?

169

What plant becomes the name of a star by removing the first letter;
becomes a number without the last letter and becomes a bird if the
first and last letters are taken away?

Answers

165
A castle.

166
A leaf.

167
A snake.

168
A hole.

169
Ivy.
VY = VY Canis Majoris, one of the largest known stars
IV = Roman numeral for 4
V = representation of a bird

Riddles

170
What work can one never finish?

171
Everyone needs this, it's great with an 'r' on the end but you're sad
when the first letter goes away. What is it?

172
Man walks over, man walks under,
In times of war he burns asunder.
What is it?

173
What's the only room from which no one can enter or leave?

174
I'm not the sort that's eaten,
I'm not the sort you bake.
Don't put me in an oven,
I don't taste that great.
But when applied correctly,
Around me you will find,
Problems are so simple,
When my digits come to mind.
What am I?

175
What can you break but not touch?

Answers

170
An autobiography.

171
Love, lover, over.

172
A bridge.

173
Mushroom.

174
Pi (3.141592653).

175
A promise.

Riddles

176

We are four against the masses. We are trying to find the one who is the whole package. We sigh, we laugh, we frown while we hope that the next one will be the one. Who are we?

177

This walks on graves at night,
Yet in homes during the day,
Men are scared of it, women like it;
Children play with it,
It lives on dates and salt,
It is covered in hair,
Its name starts with 'M'
And it's mentioned in the Quran.
What is it?

178

When I take off my clothes, it puts on its clothes.
When I put on my clothes, it takes off its clothes.
What am I?

179

If a man carried my burden,
He would break his back.
I am not rich,
But I leave silver in my track.
What am I?

Answers

176
Four orphaned siblings.

177
Moth.

178
A clothes hanger.

179
A circle.

Riddles

180

Two bodies have I, though both joined in one,
The more I stand still the faster I run.
What am I?

181

It can be cracked, it can be made,
It can be told, it can be played.
What is it?

182

What can't be burned in a fire nor drowned in water?

183

With pointed fangs it sits in wait,
With piercing force it doles out fate,
Over bloodless victims proclaiming its might,
Eternally joining in a single bite
What is it?

184

What is something to everybody and nothing to everyone else?

185

Begin with a word, five letters to my name,
Remove the first and last but I am the same
Take out my middle and still I remain.
What word am I?

Answers

180
An hourglass.

181
A joke.

182
Ice. It melts instead of burning in a fire and floats in water.

183
A stapler.

184
Your mind.

185
Empty. (mpt, emty or mt depending on your interpretation)

Riddles

186

I lack much reason, but often rhyme,
And require logic to pass the time,
To get the words to tell your kin,
Look for clues that lie within,
Though all are different, they act the same,
The answer is practically in the name.
What am I?

187

It may only be given,
Not taken or bought,
What the sinner desires,
But the saint does not.
What am I?

188

Touch me and I'm gone,
But to you I belong.
I stay with you for life,
But I am not seen by your wife.
What am I?

189

I am flora, not fauna,
I am foliage, not trees,
I am shrubbery, not grass,
What am I?

Answers

186
A riddle.

187
Forgiveness.

188
Your reflection in the water.

189
A bush.

Riddles

190

My first is in FLOWER and in ROSE
My second is in FORK and well as HOSE
My third is in CROCUS but not in GNOME
My fourth is in RAKE never in HOME
My fifth is in HOE and also in WEEDS
My sixth is in SHEARS though not in SEEDS
My seventh is in LADYBIRD not in CREATURE
What am I?

191

Destroyer of the unbreakable,
More of me is hidden than seen.
What am I?

192

I saw a strange creature,
Long, hard, and straight,
Thrusting in a round, dark, opening,
Preparing to discharge its load of lives,
Puffing and squealing noises accompanied it,
Then a final screech as it slowed and stopped.
What am I?

193

What goes around and in the house,
but never touches the house?

Answers

190
Rockery.

191
An iceberg.

192
A subway train.

193
The sun.

Riddles

194

I am pronounced as one letter
But written as three,
There are two of me,
I am single, I am double,
I can be blue, brown, black or green.
I can be read from right to left or left to right
And am still the same.
What am I?

195

I'm a six letter word. If I did not exist, you wouldn't either. With my
first letter omitted I'm an alternative. The last three letters are
feminine. The first four letters make an insect.
What word am I?

196

What kind of a nut has a hole?

197

Many foods can make me strong but give me water and I won't
last long. What am I?

198

I am a five letter word. If you remove my last four letters I am still
pronounced the same. What word am I?

Answers

194
Eye.

195
Mother.
other = an alternative
her = feminine
moth = an insect

196
A donut.

197
Fire.

198
Queue.

Riddles

199

I am something everybody tends to overlook, no matter how careful they are. What am I?

200

I am too much for one, enough for two, but nothing to three. What am I?

201

Take away my first letter and I remain the same. Take away my last letter and I remain unchanged. Remove all my letters and I'm still me. What am I?

202

There was a girl in our town,
Silk an' satin was her gown,
Silk an' satin, gold an' velvet,
Guess her name, three times I've telled it.

203

As soft as silk, as white as milk,
As bitter as gall, a thick green wall,
And a green coat covers me all.
What am I?

204

Long legs, crooked thighs, little head and no eyes.
What am I?

Answers

199
Your nose.

200
A secret.

201
A mail carrier.

202
Ann.

203
A walnut.

204
A pair of tongs.

Riddles

205

Make three fourths of a cross, and a circle complete;
And let two semicircles on a perpendicular meet;
Next add a triangle that stands on two feet;
Next two semicircles, and a circle complete.
What am I?

206

Flour of England, fruit of Spain,
Met together in a shower of rain;
Put in a bag tied round with a string,
If you'll tell me this riddle, I'll give you a ring.
What am I?

207

Thirty white horses upon a red hill,
Now they tramp, now they champ, now they stand still.
What are we?

208

Formed long ago, yet made to-day,
Employed while others sleep;
What few would like to give away,
Nor any wish to keep.
What am I?

209

What walks all day on its head?

Answers

205
Tobacco.

206
A plum-pudding.

207
Your teeth.

208
A bed.

209
A nail in a horseshoe.

Riddles

210

Lives in winter, dies in summer,
And grows with its root upwards.
What am I?

211

Two legs sat upon three legs, with one leg in his lap;
In comes four legs and runs away with one leg;
Up jumps two legs, catches up three legs,
Throws it after four legs, and makes him drop one leg.
What are we?

212

Thomas a Tattamus took two T's,
To tie two tups to two tall trees,
To frighten the terrible Thomas a Tattamus!
Tell me how many T's there are in all THAT!

213

Humpty Dumpty sat on a wall,
Humpty Dumpty had a great fall;
All the king's horses and all the king's men,
Cannot put Humpty Dumpty together again.
What am I?

214

What is round as a dishpan, deep as a tub, and
still the oceans couldn't fill it up?

Answers

210
An icicle.

211
A man, a stool, a leg of mutton, and a dog.

212
2.

213
An egg.

214
A sieve.

Riddles

215
In spring I look gay,
Decked in comely array,
In Summer more clothing I wear;
When colder it grows,
I fling off my clothes,
And in Winter quite naked appear.
What am I?

216
Riddle me, riddle me, ree;
A little man in a tree;
A stick in his hand,
A stone in his throat,
If you tell me this riddle,
I'll give you a groat.
What am I?

217
I am taken from a mine, and shut up in a wooden case,
from which I am never released,
and yet I am used by almost everybody.
What am I?

218
What is put on a table, cut, but never eaten?

Answers

215
Tree.

216
Cherry.

217
Pencil lead.

218
A pack of cards.

Riddles

219
Daffy Down Dilly
Has come to town
In a yellow petticoat
And a green gown.
What am I?

220
As I was going to St. Ives,
I met a man with seven wives,
Every wife had seven sacks,
Every sack had seven cats,
Every cat had seven kits -
Kits, cats, sacks, and wives,
How many were going to St. Ives?

Answers

219
Daffodils.

220
All potential answers to this riddle are based on its ambiguity because the riddle only tells us the group has been "met" on the journey to St. Ives and gives no further information about its intentions, only those of the narrator. As such, any one of the following answers is plausible, depending on the intention of the other party:

1: If the group that the narrator meets is assumed not to be travelling to St. Ives (this is the most common assumption), the answer would be *one* person going to St. Ives; the narrator.

2802: If the narrator met the group as they were also travelling to St. Ives (and were overtaken by the narrator, plausible given the large size of the party),the answer in this case is *all* are going to St. Ives; see below for the mathematical answer.

2800: If the narrator and the group were all travelling to St. Ives, the answer could also be *all except the narrator and the man* since the question is ambiguous about whether it is asking for the total number of entities travelling or just the number of kits, cats, sacks and wives. This would give an answer of 2,800 — 2 fewer than the answer above.

2: Two is also a plausible answer. This would involve the narrator meeting the man who is assumed to be travelling to St. Ives also, but plays on a grammatical uncertainty, since the riddle states only that the man has seven wives (and so forth), but does not explicitly mention whether the man is actually accompanied by his wives, sacks, cats, and kittens.

0: Yet another plausible answer is *zero*, once again playing on a grammatical uncertainty. The last line of the riddle states "kits, cats, sacks, wives ... were going to St. Ives?" Although the narrator clearly states he is going to St. Ives, by definition he is not one of the kits, cats, sacks, or wives, and based on the common assumption that the party was not going to St. Ives, the answer is zero.

2752: The sacks are not a person or animal and therefore cannot be in the calculation. It was not the number of things, but of "persons" the narrator met. 49 adult cats 343 kittens per wife of whom he had seven (7 × 392) = 2744 plus the seven wives 2751 plus the man 2752 persons and animals.

9: There are nine people involved, who may be going to St. Ives. The animals are all in the sacks, so they, as well as the sacks themselves, are "being taken", rather than "going".

7: There are nine people involved, who are the only ones who may be going to St. Ives, all the others "being taken" there. But since the question is limited to "Kits, cats, sacks, wives", this excludes the man and the narrator, leaving seven.

End Notes

Thank you for reading. I hope you have enjoyed all the riddles!

If you enjoyed this book, please take a moment to post a review and share with your friends. If you were unsatisfied with this book, please let me know using the contact details below.

Please send me your comments and suggestions. Any feedback is greatly appreciated.

Connect with the Author Online:

Author.JenniferEdwards@gmail.com

Made in the USA
Las Vegas, NV
25 May 2022

49359334R00056